# 56 SONGS

## YOU LIKE TO SING

ED-1596

ISBN 978-0-7935-2580-5

# G. SCHIRMER, Inc.

DISTRIBUTED BY

HAL•LEONARD
CORPORATION
7777 W. BLUEMOUND RD. P.O. BOX 13819 MILWAUKEE, WI 53213

# CONTENTS

# INDEX BY TITLE

# Allerseelen
## All Souls' Day

(Hermann von Gilm)

*English version by*
*Dr. Th. Baker*

Richard Strauss. Op. 10, № 8

Stell' auf den Tisch die duf-ten-den Re-
Be-side me set the rud-dy glow-ing

se - den, die letz-ten ro-then As-tern trag' her-bei, und lass uns
heath - er, The last au-tum-nal as-ters bring to-day, And let us

wie-der von der Lie-be re - den, wie einst im Mai.
tell a-gain of love to-geth - er, As once in May.

37700

Printed in the U.S.A. by G. Schirmer, Inc.

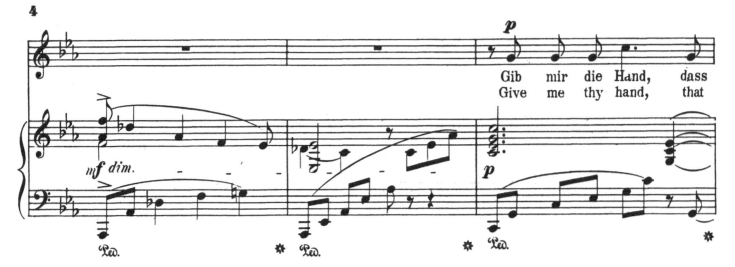

Gib mir die Hand, dass
Give me thy hand, that

ich sie heim-lich drü-cke, und wenn man's sieht, mir ist es ei-ner-lei,
I may fond-ly press it, Should oth-ers see, I care not what they say;

gib mir nur ei-nen dei-ner sü-ssen Bli-cke, wie einst im
Let one fond glance, love, fill my heart and bless it, As once in

Mai. Es blüht und duf-tet heut auf je-dem
May. On ev-'ry grave to-day sweet flow'rs are

# ALOHA OE
## FAREWELL TO THEE

Composed by H. M. QUEEN LILIUOKALANI

Moderato

Ha - a - heo    ka    u - a    i - na    pa - - li    Ke
Proud - ly swept    the    rain - cloud    by    the    cliff ____    As

nihi    a - e - la    ka - na - he - le    E    ha - ha - i    a - na    i    ka
on    it    glid - ed    through    the    trees, ____    Still    fol - low - ing    with grief    the

li - ko    Pu - a    a - hi - hi    le - hu - a - o    u - ka.
li - ko    The    a - hi - hi - le - hua    of    the    vale. ____

CHORUS.

A - lo - ha oe, a - lo - ha oe, E ke o - na - o - na no - ho i - ka li - po A
Fare-well to thee, fare-well to thee, Thou charm-ing one who dwells a-mong the bow - ers; One

fond em - brace    a ho - i    a - e au    Un - til    we meet a - gain.
fond em - brace    be - fore I now de - part,    Un - til    we meet a - gain.

**2.**

Ka halia ko aloha kai hiki mai
Ke hone ae nei i ku'u manawa
O oe no ka'u aloha
A loko e hana nei.

**2.**

Thus sweet memories come back to me,
Bringing fresh remembrance of the past;
Dearest one, yes thou art mine own,
From thee true love shall ne'er depart.

**3.**

Maopopo kuu ike ika nani
Na pua rose o Maunawili
I laila hoohie na mau u
Mikiala ika nani oia pua.

**3.**

I have seen and watched thy loveliness,
Thou sweet rose of Maunawili,
And 'tis there the birds oft love to dwell
And sip the honey from thy lips.

# Ave Maria

(Walter Scott)

German translation by
Adam Storck

English adaptation by
Dr. Theo. Baker

Franz Schubert. Op. 52, No. 6

murk - y cav - ern's air so heav - y Shall
lä - - chelst, Ro - sen-duf - te we - hen. in
et in ho - ra___ mor - tis, in

breathe of balm, if Thou hast smil'd; O Maid - en, hear a maid-en plead-ing, O
die - ser dumpfen Fel-sen-kluft; o Mut - ter, hör' des Kin-des Fle-hen, o
ho - ra mor-tis no - stræ, in ho - ra mor - tis, mor-tis no - stræ, in

Moth - er, hear a sup-pliant child! A - ve Ma-ri -
Jung-frau, ei - ne Jungfrau ruft! A - ve Ma-ri -
ho - ra mor-tis no - stræ. A - ve Ma-ri -

a!
a!
a!

A - ve Ma - ri - a! Stain - less
*A - ve Ma - ri - a!* *Rei - ne*
A - ve Ma - ri - a! gra - ti - a ple -

styl'd! Each fiend of air or earth-ly es - sence, From this their wonted haunt ex -
*Magd! Der Er - de und der Luft Dä - mo - nen, von dei - nes Au-ges Huldver-*
na, Ma - ri - a, gra - ti - a ple - na, Ma - ri - a, gra-ti - a ple -

il'd, Shall flee be-fore Thy ho - ly pres - ence! We
*jagt, sie kön - nen hier nicht bei uns woh - nen! Wir*
na. A - ve, A - ve! Do - mi-nus, Do - mi-nus tecum; Be-ne -

bow, be - neath our cares o'er-la - den, To
*woll'n uns still dem Schick - sal beu - gen, da*
di - cta tu in mu - li - e - ri-bus, et

# Barcarolle

## Belle Nuit    O Lovely Night

### From the opera "Les Contes d'Hoffmann"

*English version by*
*M. Louise Baum*

J. Offenbach

Bel - le nuit, ô
Fair - est night of

nuit d'a-mour, Sou-ris à nos i-vres - ses! Nuit plus dou-ce
star-ry ray, O smile on hap-py lov - ers! Dear-er far than

que le jour, Ô bel - le nuit d'a-mour! Le temps fuit et
e'er was day, O love-ly night, be kind! Time and tide are

sers, Ver - sez - nous vos_ bai - sers! Ah!_____
kiss! Sway - ing sea, cradle our bliss! Ah!_____

Bel - le nuit, ô nuit d'a - mour, Sou - ris_ à nos i - vres - - ses!
Fair - est night of star - ry ray, O smile on hap - py lov - - ers!

Nuit plus dou - ce que le jour, Ô bel - le nuit d'a - mour!
Dear - er far than e'er was day, O love - ly night, be kind!

O bel - le nuit d'a - mour! Ah! Sou - ris à nos i - vres - -
O thou night of love! Ah! Love - ly night, be kind!_____

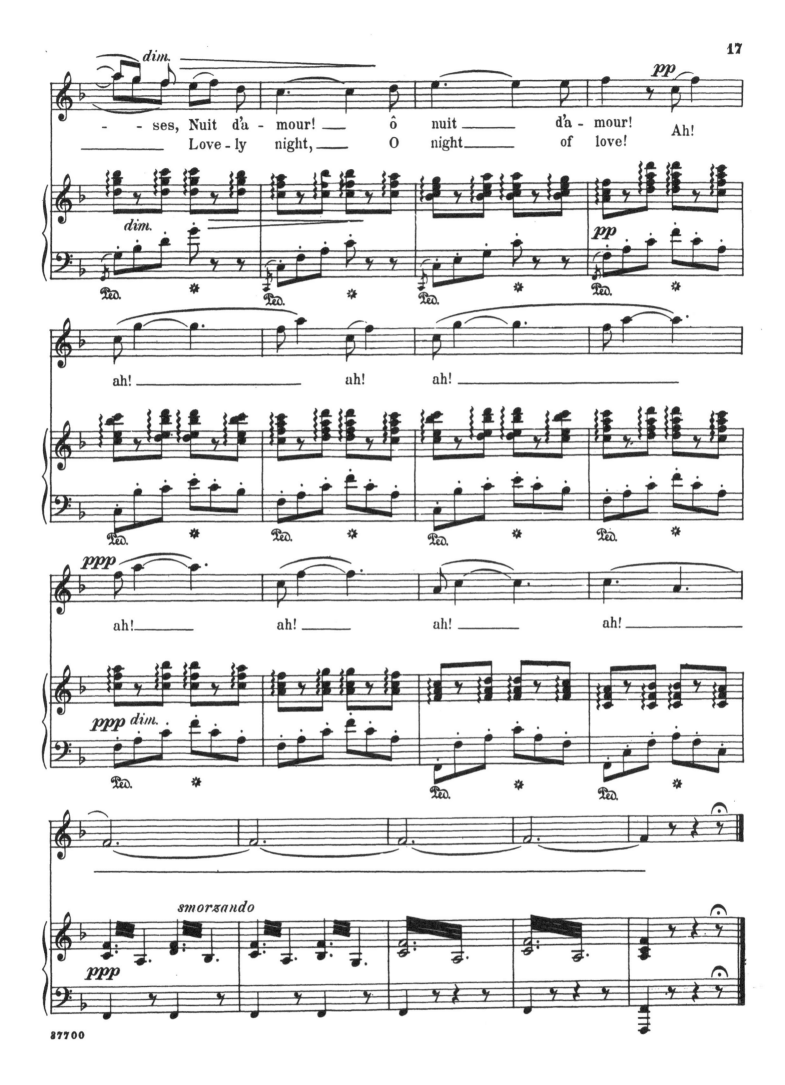

# Beau Soir
(Paul Bourget)

## Evening Fair

English version by
Henry G. Chapman

Claude Debussy

blé,_____ Un conseil d'être heu - reux semble sor - tir des
grain,_____ A be-hest to be glad, that seems from all things

cho - ses Et mon - ter vers le cœur_ trou -
stream - ing, Doth a - rise to my heart_ in

blé. Un con - seil de goû-ter le char - me d'être au
pain. A be - hest to ex-plore the ut - most joy of

mon - de, Ce - pen - dant qu'on est jeune et que le soir est
be - ing, In this day of my youth, the while the eve-ning's

# Still wie die Nacht
## Calm as the Night

English version by
Nathan Haskell Dole

Carl Bohm

87700

soll dei - ne Lie - be, dei - ne Lie - be sein,___
Should be thy love, should be thy love___ for me,___

soll dei - ne Lie - be sein!
should be thy love___ for me!

Wenn du mich liebst
If love like mine

so wie ich dich,___ will ich dein ei - -gen
glow in thy heart,___ I am for ev - - -er

sein. / thine.

Heiss____ wie der Stahl,____ und / Fer- -vent as steel,____ and

fest wie der Stein____ soll dei - ne Lie - be, dei - ne / firm as the hills, Should be thy love, should be thy

Lie- -be sein,____ soll dei - ne Lie - -be / love____ for me,____ should be thy love____ for

sein!____ / me!____

# Carry me back to old Virginny

## Song and Chorus

Words and Music by
James A. Bland

87700

There's where the old dark-ey's heart am longed to go.　There's where I la-bored so
There's where this old dark-ey's life will pass a-way.　Mas - sa and mis-sis have

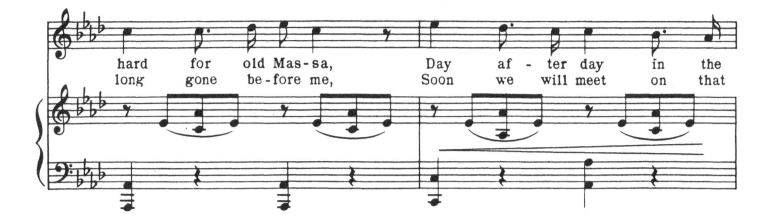

hard　　for old Mas-sa,　　Day　af - ter day　in　the
long　gone　be-fore me,　Soon　we　will meet　on　that

field　of yel - low　corn,　　No　place　on earth　do　I
bright and gold-en　shore.　　There　we'll　be hap - py and

love more sin-cere-ly　　Than　old　Vir - gin - ny, the__ state where I　was born.
free from all sor-row,　There's where we'll meet and we'll　nev - er part no more.

*rit.*

87700

**Refrain**

There's where the birds war-ble sweet in the spring-time,

There's where the birds war-ble sweet in the spring-time,

There's where the birds war-ble sweet in the spring-time,

There's where the birds war-ble sweet in the spring-time,

*rit.*

There's where this old dark-ey's heart am longed to go.

There's where this old dark-ey's heart am longed to go.

There's where this old dark-ey's heart am longed to go.

There's where this old dark-ey's heart am longed to go.

37700

*Repeat refrain pp after 2nd verse*

Edited by Max Spicker
English version by
Henry G. Chapman

# Wiegenlied
(Karl Simrock)
## Cradle-Song

Johannes Brahms
Op.49, No.4

Zart bewegt
*Dolce, con moto*

Gu - ten A - bend, gut' Nacht, mit
So good-night now once more, With

Ro - sen be - dacht, mit Näg-lein be - steckt, schlüpf' un - ter die
ros - es roof'd o'er, — All tied up with bows, Slip un - der the

Deck': Mor - gen früh, wenn Gott will, wirst du wie - der ge -
clothes, When the morn - ing shall break, Please the Lord, thou wilt

weckt, mor - gen früh, wenn Gott will, wirst du wie - der ge - weckt!
wake, When the morn - ing shall break, Please the Lord, thou wilt wake!

Gu - ten A - bend, gut' Nacht, von _
Good - night then once more, By _

Eng - lein be - wacht, die zei - gen im _ Traum dir _ Christ-kind - leins
an - gels watch'd o'er, _ In _ dreams thou shalt see A _ fair Christ - mas -

Baum: Schlaf' nun se - lig und süss, schau' im Traum 's Pa - ra -
tree. Go to sleep, close thine eyes, Thou shalt see Par - a -

dies! schlaf' nun se - lig und süss, schau' im Traum 's Pa - ra - dies!
dise, Go to sleep, close thine eyes, Thou shalt see Par - a - dise!

# Caro mio ben

## Dearest, believe

Edited by Carl Deis

Giuseppe Giordani
(Called "Giordanello" — 1744-1798)

Ca - ro mio ben, cre - di - mi al-men, sen - za di te lan - gui-sce il cor, —
Dear-est, be-lieve, When we must part, Lone-ly I grieve, In — my poor heart!

Ca - ro mio ben, sen - za di te lan - gui - sce il cor.
When we must part, Sad-ly I grieve, In my lone - ly heart!

Il tuo fe - del so - spi-ra o-gnor.
Thy faith-ful slave, Hear him but sigh,

Ces - sa, cru - del, tan - to ri - gor! Ces - sa, cru - del, tan - to ri - gor,
Haste then and save Him ere he die! Haste then and save, Haste then and save him,

tan - to ri - gor! Ca - ro mio ben, cre - di-mi al-men, sen - za di te___ lan -
Else he must die. Dear-est, be-lieve, When we must part, Sad - ly I grieve, In my

gui - sce il cor; ca - ro mio ben, cre - di-mi al-men, sen - za di te_____
lone - ly heart! Dear-est, be-lieve, When we must part, Lone - ly I grieve,___

___ lan - gui - sce il cor!
___ In my poor heart!

# Widmung.

## Dedication.

(Wolfgang Müller.)

Edited by
Max Spicker

Robert Franz

Op 14, No 1.

**Andante con moto.**
*Innig.* Con affetto.

O dan - ke nicht für die - se Lie - der, mir ziemt es, dank - bar Dir zu sein; Du gabst sie mir,___ ich ge - be wie - der, was jetzt und einst und e - wig Dein.

Nay, thank me not that songs I sing thee, Thanks there shall be, but they'll be mine! 'Twas thou that gav'st,___ I do but bring thee What was and ev - er shall be thine.

Dein sind sie al - le ja ge - we - sen, aus Dei - ner
I've look'd in thy dear eyes, and tak - en The truth that

lie - ben Au - gen Licht hab' ich sie treu - lich ab - ge -
there a - lone be - longs; Then tell me not, I was mis -

le - sen, kennst Du die eig - nen Lie - der
tak - en, Dost thou not know - nen thine own sweet

nicht? kennst Du die eig - nen Lie - der nicht?
songs? Dost thou not know - nen thine own sweet songs?

(Henry G. Chapman.)

*Dedicated to Modest P. Moussorgsky*

# A Dissonance

## Romance

English version by
Kurt Schindler

Words and Music by
A. Borodine
(1868)

Thy lips say, "I love thee, be-

lieve me," And yet, in the sound of thy

voice          A false note rings,     that doth grieve me,                    It

is    in thy smile,    in thine eyes!          Thou know'st,   thou canst not   de-

ceive me!

# "La donna è mobile"
## "Woman so changeable"
### Canzone from the Opera
### "RIGOLETTO"

English version by
Sigmund Spaeth

Giuseppe Verdi

ma - bi - le,　leg - gia - dro vi - so,　in pian - to o in ri - so,　è men - zo-
am - ia - ble,　Al - ways be - guil - ing,　Tear - ful or smil - ing,　Still a de-

gne - ro.　La_ don - na è mo - bil　qual_ piu - ma al　ven - to,　mu - ta d'ac-
ceiv - er!　Wo - man ca - pri - cious,　Swayed like a　feath - er!　None can tell

cen - to　e__ di pen - sier,　　　　　　　　　　　　　　e__ di pen-
wheth - er　He__ should be - lieve!　　　　　　　　　　　　Should he be-

sier,　　　e,_____
lieve?　　　Ah!_____

con forza

e___ di pen - sier.
Should he be - lieve?

E sem - pre mi - se - ro chi a lei s'af-
Lo, how great mis-er-y With him a -

fi - da, chi le con - fi - da, mal-cau-to il co - re! Pur mai non
bid - eth, Who-so con - fid - eth In all her grac - es! But true fe -

sen - te - si fe - li - ce ap - pie - no chi su quel se - no
li - ci - ty By him is wast - ed Who ne'er hath tast - ed

non li-ba-a-mo-re! La\_don-na è mo-bil qual\_piu-ma\_al
Love's fond em-brac-es! Light-heart-ed wo-man, Swayed like a

ven-to, mu-ta d'ac-cen-to e\_di pen-sier,
feath-er! None can tell wheth-er He\_should be-lieve.

e\_\_ di pen-sier, e,_____
Should he be-lieve? Ah!_____

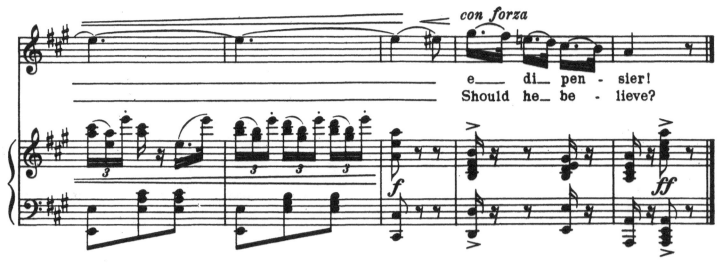

e\_ di pen-sier!
Should he\_ be-lieve?

# "Do not go, my love"

Words by
Sir Rabindranath Tagore

*Music by
Richard Hageman

*Orchestral score and parts may be obtained from the publisher.

87700

I fear lest I lose you when I am sleep-

-ing. Do not go, my love,

with-out ask-ing my leave.

Più mosso

I start up and stretch my

*ff* *pp subito* *dolce*

*tenuto*

hands _____ to touch you. I ask my-

self, "Is it a dream?"_____

self, "Is it a dream?"_____

**Tempo I° Più mosso**

Could I but en-

tan - gle your feet with my heart, and hold them

fast        to        my        breast!

Adagio

*rall. molto*

*pp*

Do        not

Ped.                                                                          ✽

go,        my love,        with-out ask-ing my        leave.

*m.s.*                                                                    *m.s.*

*rall.*                                                        *pp*

Ped.                                                        Ped.            ✽

# Träume

## Dreams

Poem by
**Mathilde Wesendonk**
**English version by**
**Grace Hall**

Music by
Richard Wagner

**Sehr mässig bewegt, aber nie schleppend**
In very moderate time, but never dragging

Piano

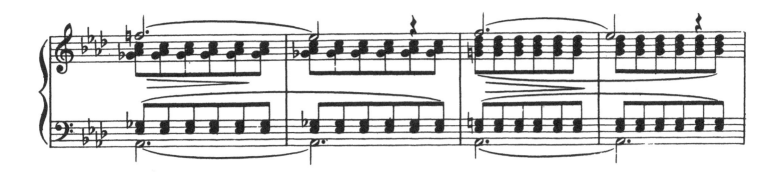

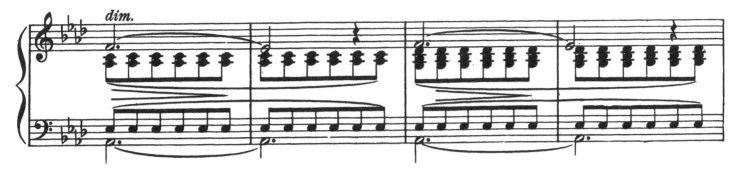

37700

Sag', welch' wun-der-ba - re Träu - me
Dreams of mys-tic-al en-chant - ment

hal - ten mei-nen Sinn um-fan - gen,
hold my spir-it fast in bond - age,

dass sie nicht wie lee - re Schäu - me sind in
dreams that from the void e-merg - ing sink no

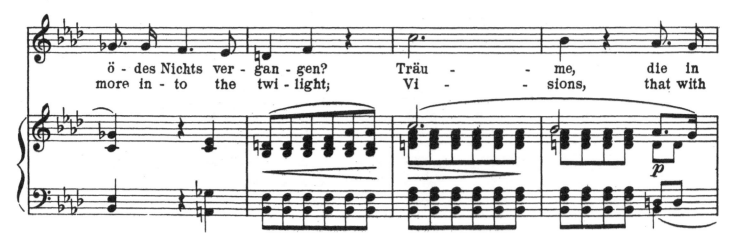

ö - des Nichts ver-gan - gen? Träu - me, die in
more in-to the twi-light; Vi - sions, that with

je - der Stun - de, je - dem Ta - ge schö - ner blüh'n, und mit ih - rer
ev - 'ry hour to great - er won - der grow and ev - er with heav'n - ly

Him-mels-kun - de se - lig durch's Ge - mü - the zieh'n?
ma - gic draw the soul to high - er ec - sta - sy.

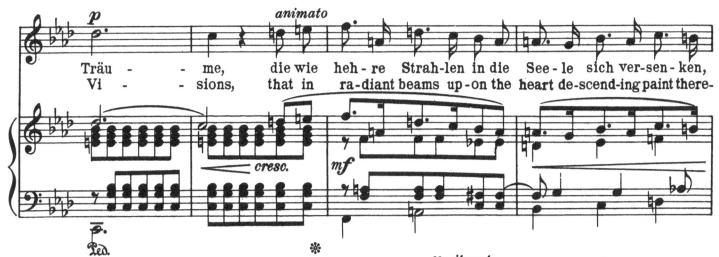

Träu - me, die wie heh - re Strah-len in die See - le sich ver-sen - ken,
Vi - sions, that in ra-diant beams up-on the heart de-scend-ing paint there-

dort ein e - wig Bild zu ma - len: All - ver-ges - sen, Ein-ge-den - ken!
on a fair e - ter - nal im - age, nev - er fad - ing, still re-mem - bered.

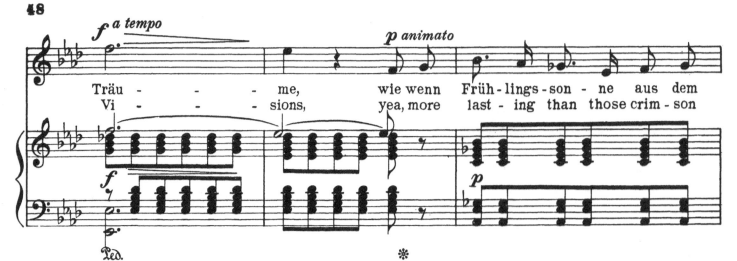

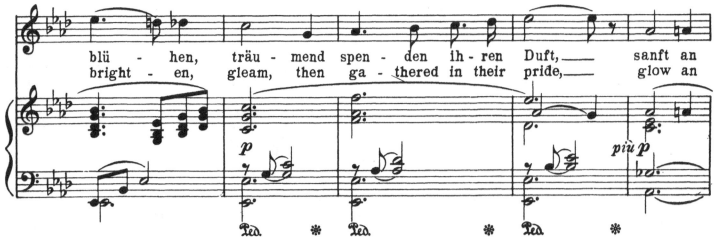

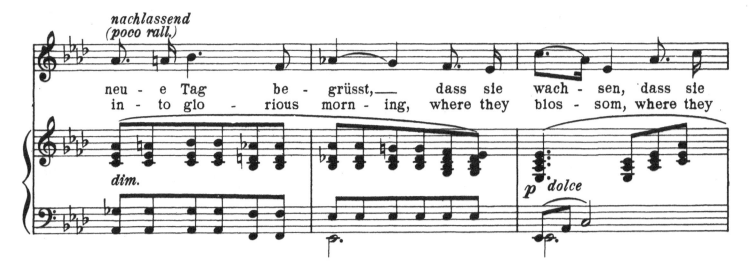

dei - ner Brust ver-glü - hen, und dann sin-ken in die
hour up - on thy bo - som, and then fad - ed fall to

*morendo*

Gruft.
dust.

*pp*

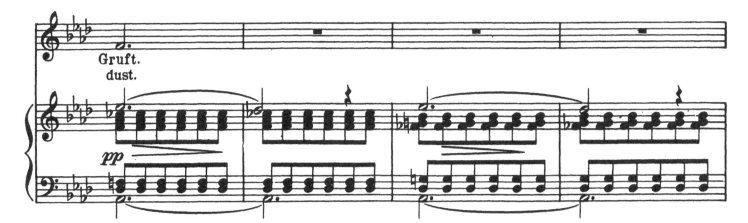

*più p*

*pp*

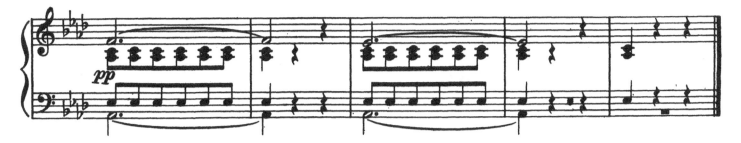

37700

# "Drink to me only with thine eyes"

OLD ENGLISH AIR
Date uncertain

BEN JONSON
(1573 - 1637)

Very smoothly, and rather slow

Drink to me on - ly  with thine eyes, And I__ will pledge with mine,__

Or leave a kiss with - in__ the cup,__ And I'll__ not ask  for  wine;___ The

thirst_ that from the soul_ doth rise, Doth ask a drink di - vine,__

But might I of Jove's nec - tar sip, __ I would not change for

thine!

I sent thee late a ros - y wreath, Not so__ much hon'- ring thee __

As giv - ing it a hope that there— It could not with - er'd

be; ____ But thou_there - on didst on - ly breathe And

sent'st it back to me; ____ Since when it grows, and

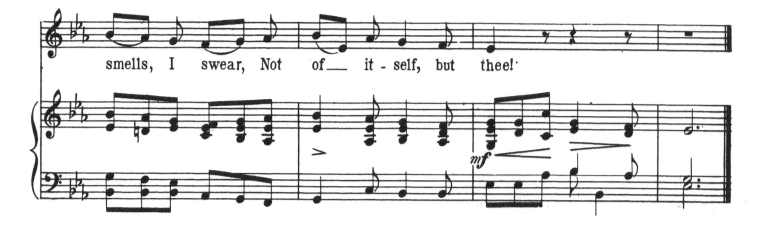

smells, I swear, Not of___ it - self, but thee!

# Élégie

English version by
CHARLOTTE H. COURSEN

J. Massenet

tant mon bonheur,_____ Ô bien - ai - mé, tu t'en es__ al - lé! Et c'est en
joy from my heart,_____ Loved one, how far from my life hast thou flown! Vain - ly to

vain que revient le prin-temps! Oui, sans re - tour, a - vec toi le gai soleil,
me does the springtime re-turn! It brings thee nev - er a-gain: Dark is the sun!

Les jours riants sont par - tis! Comme en mon cœur tout est sombre et gla - cé! Tout est flé -
Dead are the days of de-light! Cold is my heart and as dark as the grave! Life is in

tri! _____ Pour _____ tou - jours! _____
vain _____ ev - - er - more! _____

# Good-bye!

G. J. White-Melville

F. P. Tosti
Edited by Carl Deis

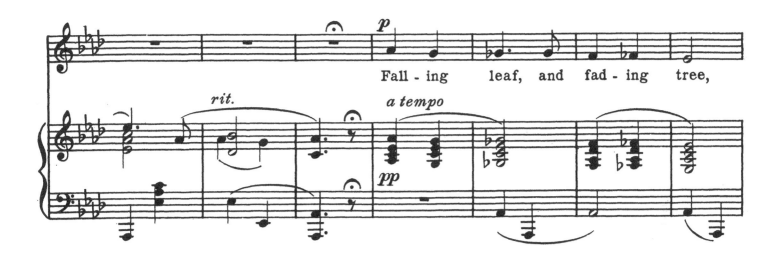

37700

you and me, shad-ows ris - ing on you and me. The

swal - lows are mak - ing them read - y to fly, Wheel - ing

*rit.*        *pp lentamente*

out on a wind - y___ sky.___ Good - bye, Sum - mer! Good-

*lentamente*        *col canto*        *pp*

*cresc.*        *rit.*

bye, Good - bye! Good - bye, sum - mer! Good - bye, Good -

*cresc.*        *col canto*

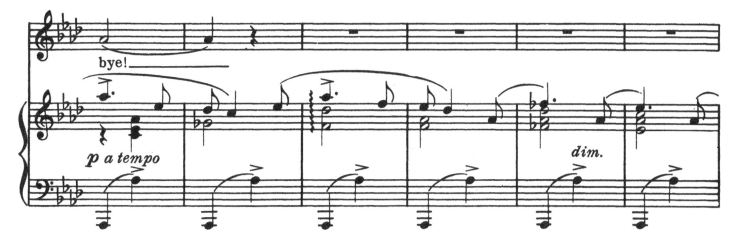

bye!

*p a tempo* — *dim.*

*pp poco più mosso*
*parlato* — *molto rall.* _ _ _ _

Hush! A voice from the far a - way!

*pp poco più mosso* — *molto rall.* _ _ _ _

"Lis-ten and learn," it seems_ to say, "All the to - mor-rows shall

be as to - day, All the to - mor - rows shall be as to -

day." The cord is frayed, the cruse is dry. The

link must break, and the lamp must die._____ Good-

bye, to Hope! Good-bye, Good-bye! Good-bye, to

Hope! Good - bye, Good - bye!_____

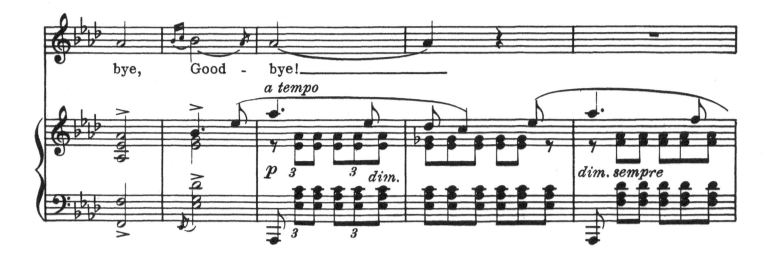

# Habanera

from the opera
## "Carmen"

English version by
Dr. Th. Baker

Georges Bizet

fait, me - nace ou pri - è - re, L'un par - le bien, l'au - tre se
vails, nei - ther threat nor prayer, One speaks me fair, __ the __ oth - er

*portando*

tait; Et c'est l'au - tre que je pré - fè - re, Il n'a rien
sighs, 'Tis the oth - er whom I pre - fer: Tho' mute, his

*espress.*

dit, __ mais il me plaît. __ L'a - mour! __
heart to __ mine re - - plies. __ Oh Love! __

l'a - mour! __ l'a - mour! __
Oh Love! __ Oh Love! __

l'a - mour! L'a-mour est en - fant de Bo - hê - me, Il n'a ja -
Oh Love! A Gyp-sy boy is Love, 'tis true, He ev - er

mais, ja-mais con-nu de loi, Si tu ne m'ai-mes pas, je t'ai - me; Si
was and ev-er will be free; Tho' you may love me not, I love___ you, If

je t'ai - me, prends garde à toi!_____ Si tu ne m'ai-mes pas, si
I love you, be-ware of me!_____ Tho' you may love me not, tho'

tu ne m'ai-mes pas, je t'ai - me! Mais si je t'ai-me, si je
you may love me not, I love you! But if I love you, if I

t'ai-me, prends garde___ à toi!___
love you, be-ware___ of me!___

L'oi-seau que tu croy-ais sur-pren-dre Bat-tit de l'aîle et___ s'en-vo-
Will you fol-low a bird to net him, On buoy-ant wing a-way he

la; L'a-mour est loin, tu peux l'at-ten-dre; Tu ne l'at-tends plus, il est
soars; Love is war-y when you a-wait him: A-wait him not,___ and he is

là! Tout au-tour de toi vi-te, vi-te, Il vient, s'en va,___ puis il re-
yours! All a-round you he swift-ly sweeps, Now here, now there he___ light-ly

*portando*

vient; Tu crois le te - nir, il t'é - vi - te; Tu crois l'é - vi - ter, il te
flies; When you deem him yours, he es - capes, You'd fain es - cape, and you are

tient!\_\_\_\_\_ L'a - mour!\_\_\_\_\_ l'a -
his!\_\_\_\_\_ Oh Love!\_\_\_\_\_ Oh

mour!\_\_\_\_\_ l'a - mour!\_\_\_\_\_ l'a -
Love!\_\_\_\_\_ Oh Love!\_\_\_\_\_ Oh

*p*

mour! L'a-mour est en - fant de Bo - hê-me, Il n'a ja - mais, ja-mais con-nu de
Love! A Gyp-sy boy is Love, 'tis true, He ev - er was and ev - er will be

loi,      Si  tu  ne  m'ai - mes  pas,  je  t'ai - me;      Si
free;     Tho' you  may  love  me  not,  I  love_____ you,  If

je  t'ai - me,  prends  garde  à  toi!_____      Si  tu  ne
I  love you,  be - ware  of  me!_____      Tho' you  may

*f*     *pp*

m'ai - mes  pas,  si  tu  ne  m'ai - mes  pas,  je  t'ai - me!
love  me · not,  tho'  you  may  love  me  not,  I  love  you!

*f*

*cresc.*     *f*     3

Mais  si  je  t'ai - me,  si  je  t'ai - me,  prends garde  à__  toi!_____
But  if  I  love you,  if  I  love you,  be - ware  of__  me!_____

*pp*     *cresc.*     *f*     *ff*

# I love you
## Ich liebe dich

Poem by Herrosee
English version by
Lorraine Noel Finley

Ludwig van Beethoven
Edited by Carl Deis

37700

thus may God who reigns a-bove, And hears my heart con- fess- ing, Pro-
Got - tes Se - gen ü - ber dir, du mei - nes Le - bens Freu - de, Gott

tect you, dear, with all His love, And grant us both His bless-ing, Pro-
schü - tze dich, er - halt' dich mir, schütz' und er - halt' uns Bei - de, Gott

tect you, dear, with all His love, And grant us both His bless-ing, And
schü - tze dich, er - halt' dich mir, schütz' und er-halt' uns Bei - de, er-

grant us both His bless-ing, And grant His bless - ing!
halt', er-halt' uns Bei - de, er - halt' uns Bei - de.

# „Ich liebe dich"
## "I love thee"

German words translated from the Danish by
F. von Holstein.

English version by
Henry G. Chapman

Edvard Grieg

Glück ist die - ses Herz ge - weiht;
good a - lone this heart shall be;

wie Gott auch
For to what -

mag des Le - bens Schick - sal len - ken, ich lie - be dich, ich
ev - er fate God's will may doom me, I love thee, dear, I

lie - be dich, ich lie - be dich in Zeit und E - wig - keit! Ich
love thee, dear, I love thee now and for e - ter - ni - ty, I

lie - be dich in Zeit und E - wig - keit!
love thee now and for e - ter - ni - ty!

# Júrame
## Promise, Love
### Spanish Tango

English version by
Frederick H. Martens

Words and Music by
Maria Grever

toy cer - ca de tí y es-tás con - ten - to, No qui - sie - ra que de na - die te a - cor -
geth-er, hearts in hap-pi-ness ce - ment-ed, In your mem-'ry thought of oth - ers I'd have

*ten.*

dá - ras; Ten - go ce - los has-ta del pen-sa-mien-to Que pue - da re - cor -
per-ish, E - ven thoughts make me jeal-ous, dis - con - tent-ed, Be-cause they may re -

dar-te a o-tra mu-jer a - ma-da. Jú - ra - me_____ que aun que pa - se mu-cho
call some oth-er girl whom you cher-ish. Prom-ise, love,_____ that your heart, the years de-

tiem-po No ol-vi-da-rás el mo - men-to, En que yo te co-no-cí. Mí-ra-me,_____
fy - ing, Will re-call that hour un - dy-ing When we first swore to be true. Trust me, love,_____

* These bracketed notes are not sung in the second stanza.

# The Lass with the Delicate Air

### Song

*Soprano, or Tenor*

Edited by Max Spicker

Michael Arne
(1740 or 1741 - 1786)

37700

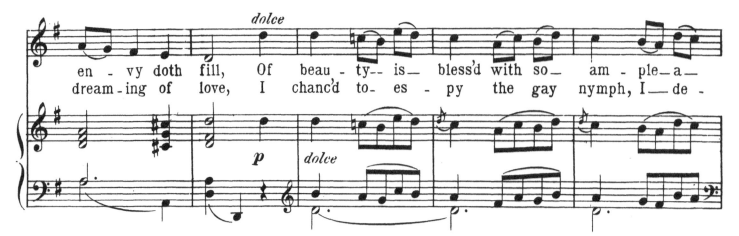

en - vy doth fill, Of beau - ty - is - bless'd with so - am - ple a -
dream - ing of love, I chanc'd to - es - py the gay nymph, I - de -

share, Men call her - the - lass with the del - i - cate air, with the
clare, And real - ly - she had a most del - i - cate air, a most

del - - - - - i-cate air, - Men call - her - the lass with the -
del - - - - - i-cate air, - And real - ly - she had a - most

del - i - cate air.
del - i - cate air.

*) 2. One

*) This verse may be omitted.

3. By a mur-mur-ing—— brook on a green moss-y——

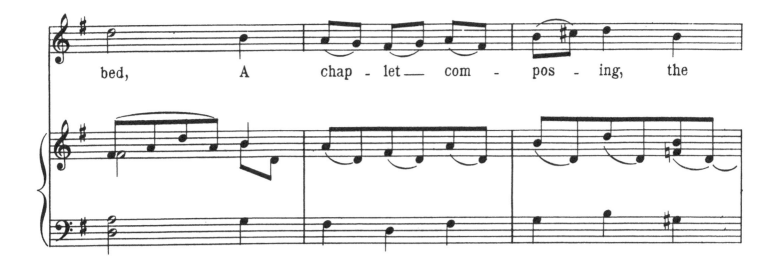

bed, A chap-let—— com - pos - ing, the

fair—— one was laid; Sur - pris'd and—— trans - port-ed—— I——

could not\_ for - bear,\_ With rap - ture\_ to\_ gaze on her

del - i - cate air, on her del - - - - -

- i - cate air,\_ with rap - ture to\_ gaze on\_ her\_

del _ i _ cate air.

4. A thou - sand times— o'er I've re - peat - ed— my— suit, But

still— the— tor - men - tor af - fects to be mute! Then tell me,— ye—

87700

swains who have con-quer'd the fair,— How to win the dear lass with the

*p*  *con tenerezza*

del - i - cate air, with the del - - - - i-cate air,— How to

*cresc. e rit.*  *p*

lass— with the— del - i - cate

*cresc.*  *p*

win— the— dear lass with the— del - i - cate air.

*cresc.*  *col canto*  *p*

# The Last Rose of Summer

## Qui sola vergin rosa

Thomas Moore

Old Irish Air*
Piano accompaniment by Carl Deis

*Used by Friedrich von Flotow
in his famous opera "Martha".

87700

3. So__ soon may__ I__ fol - low When friend - ships de - cay, And from
2. Per - chè so - la i - gno - ra - ta Lan - guir__ nel tuo giar - din, Dal__

*a tempo*

*mp sempre arpeggiando*

love's shin - ing__ cir - cle The__ gems__ drop a - way. When__
ven - to__ tor - men - ta - ta In__ pre - da a un rio des - tin? Sul__

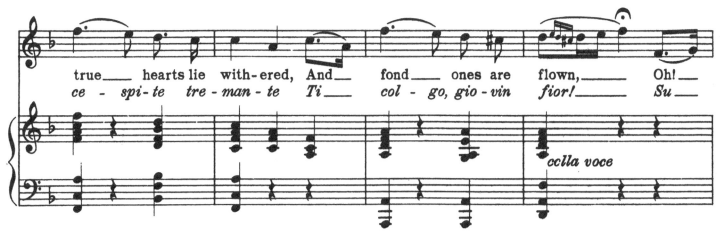

true__ hearts lie with - ered, And__ fond__ ones are flown,__ Oh!__
ce - spi - te tre - man - te Ti__ col - go, gio - vin fior!__ Su__

*colla voce*

who would in - hab - it This__ bleak__ world a - lone?
que - sto__ co - re a - man - te Co - si__ mor - rai d'a - mor.

# Lilacs

(Kath. Beketoff)

English version by
Henry G. Chapman

Sergei Rachmaninoff. Op. 21, Nº 5

**Allegretto**

*sempre tranquillo*

**Voice**

**Piano**

Morning skies    are a-glow
Mor-gen - rot    schon er-glüht,

*p*

*un poco ten.*

While the li - lac - trees blow,
und der Flie-der-busch blüht,

And I breathe of the fresh morning
und ich at - me so frisch Mor-gen-

*mf cantabile*

wind;
wind;

*p*

By the shad-ow - y pool,
nach dem schatt'gen Ge-büsch,

*p*

*mf*

Where it's dew - y and cool,    I must see if my for-tune I'll
das  von Tau-trop-fen frisch,    schau' ich, ob dort mein Glück ich nicht

find.
find'.

Ah,    of luck there's scant dole,_____ Yet it's ev-'ry-one's
Ja,    des Glücks gibt's nicht viel,_____ und doch ist's al - ler

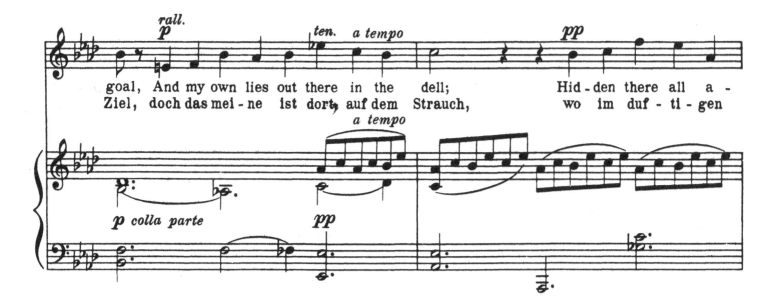

goal, And my own lies out there in the dell; Hid-den there all a-
Ziel, doch das mei-ne ist dort, auf dem Strauch, wo im duf-ti-gen

round Cluster'd li-lacs are found, And my own lit-tle for - tune, as
Grün li-la Trauben er-blühn, und mein ar-mes Glück blü - het da

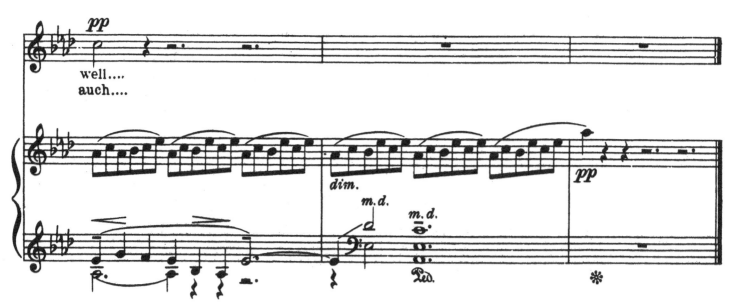

well....
auch....

# Would God I were the tender apple-blossom

Katharine Tynan Hinkson

Londonderry Air
Arranged by Harrison Niel

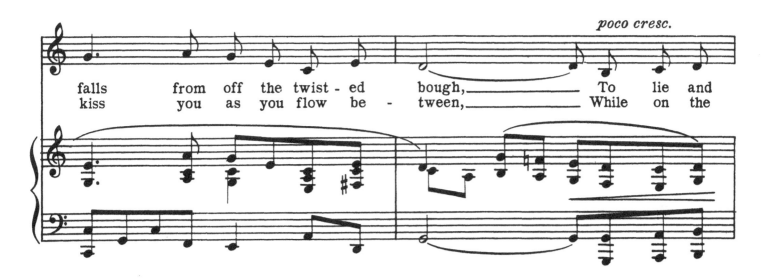

Printed in the U.S.A. by G. Schirmer, Inc.

pluck   me  glid - ing  by  so  cold,_____ While sun and
dai - sy  in  the  gar - den  path;_____ That so your

shade     your  robe  of  lawn  will  dap - ple,\_\_\_\_\_ Your  robe  of
sil - ver  foot might press me  go - ing,\_\_\_\_\_ Might press me

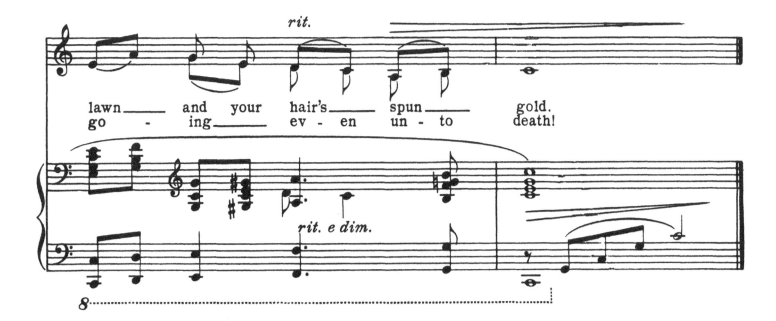

lawn\_\_\_\_\_ and  your  hair's\_\_\_\_\_ spun\_\_\_\_\_ gold.
go - ing\_\_\_\_\_ ev - en  un - to  death!

# The Lost Chord

Adelaide A. Procter

Arthur Sullivan

87700

what I was dream-ing then, But I struck one chord of mu-sic Like the

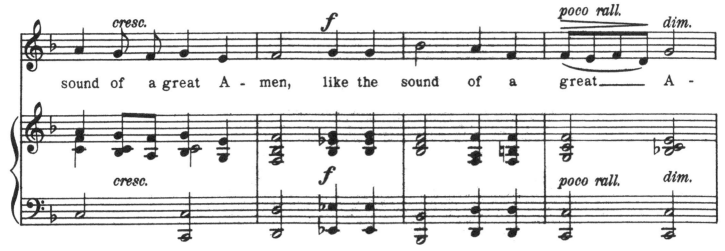

sound of a great A - men, like the sound of a great_____ A -

men. It

flood - ed the crim-son twi-light Like the close of an an-gel's Psalm, And it

lay on my fe-ver'd spir - it With a touch of__ in-fin-ite calm; It

qui-et-ed pain and sor-row Like love o-ver-com-ing strife, It

seem'd the har-mo-nious e - cho From our dis-cord-ant life. It

link'd all per-plex-ed mean-ings, In-to one per - fect peace, And

# Love's Old, Sweet Song

Words by
G. Clifton Bingham

J. L. Molloy

37700

Printed in the U.S.A. by G. Schirmer, Inc.

And in the dusk where fell the fire-light gleam, Soft-ly it wove it-self in - to our dream.

*p a tempo*

Just a song at twi-light, when the lights are low, And the flick-'ring shadows

soft-ly come and go, Tho' the heart be wea-ry, sad the day and long,

Still to us at twi - light comes Love's old song, comes Love's old sweet song.

E - ven to-day we hear Love's song of yore, Deep in our hearts it dwells for e - ver-more

Foot-steps may fal-ter, weary grow the way, Still we can hear it at the close of day.

So till the end, when life's dim shadows fall, Love will be found the sweetest song of all.

# Lullaby
## from the opera "Jocelyn"

English version by
Nathan Haskell Dole

Benjamin Godard

cealed in this re - treat, Where - to we have been led, By
chés dans cet a - sile où Dieu nous a con - duits U -

sore mis-for-tune joined, While wea - ry nights have fled, In vis-ions
nis par le mal - heur, Du - rant les lon - gues nuits Nous re - po -

87700

calm and sweet, We to - geth - er have slum-bered, Or have prayed, While a -
sons tous deux en-dor - mis sous leurs voi - les Ou pri - ons aux re -

**Andante**

bove us spark-led stars un - num - bered! Oh! wake not yet from out thy
gards des trem-blan-tes é - toi - les! Oh! ne t'é-veil - le pas en -

dream, _____ Which guard-ian an-gels have at - tend - ed,
core, _____ Pour qu'un bel an-ge de ton rê - ve

And while the gold - en splen-dors gleam _____ Still sleep, _____ my _____
En dé - rou-lant son long fil d'or, _____ En - fant, _____ per -

love, un-til 'tis end - ed. Sleep! sleep!_ Not yet ap-pears the
met-te qu'il s'a-chè - ve! Dors! Dors!_ le jour à peine a

day! Ho - ly Vir - gin, guard, guard her I pray!
lui! Vier - ge sain - te, veil - lez sur_ lui!

Andantino

Quasi Recit.

Be-neath th'Al-might-y's wing, Far from mor - tal_
Sous l'ai - le du Sei-gneur loin du bruit_ de la

knowing We hide, while like a tide, A sa-cred tide is
fou - le Et comme un flot sa - cré qui dou-ce-ment s'é-

a tempo

p
pp

flow - ing. Day af-ter day we see for - ev - er glide a - way.
cou - le Nous a-vons vu les jours pas - ser a - près les jours

Still we pray that he may pro-tect us while we bide.____
Sans ja-mais nous las - ser d'im-plo-rer son se - cours!____

Andante

Oh! wake not yet from out thy dream,____ Which guard-ian an-gels have at-
Oh! ne t'é-veil-le pas en - core____ Pour qu'un bel an-ge de ton

l.h.

pp

tend - ed,    And while the gold-en splen-dors gleam____ Still
rê - ve    En dé-rou-lant son long fil d'or,____ En-

*cresc.*    *f* *rall.* *p*    *a tempo*

sleep,____ my__ love, un-til 'tis end - - ed.
fant,____ per - met-te qu'il s'a-chè - - ve.

*cresc.*    *rall.* *pp*    *a tempo*

Sleep!    sleep!__    Not yet ap-pears the day!
Dors!    Dors!__    le jour à peine a lui.

*pp*

Ho - ly    Vir - gin, guard, guard    her I    pray.
Vier - ge    sain - te, veil - lez    sur__    lui!

*pp*

# Mother-Love

English version by
Dr. Th. Baker

H. Voigt. Op. 148
Arranged by Carl Deis

dream I yet re-mem-ber A hap-py time now far a-way When still a

moth-er's gaz-es ten-der Watch'd o-ver ev-'ry youth-ful joy. O

Moth - er faith - ful, Moth - er kind, How fond - ly bear I

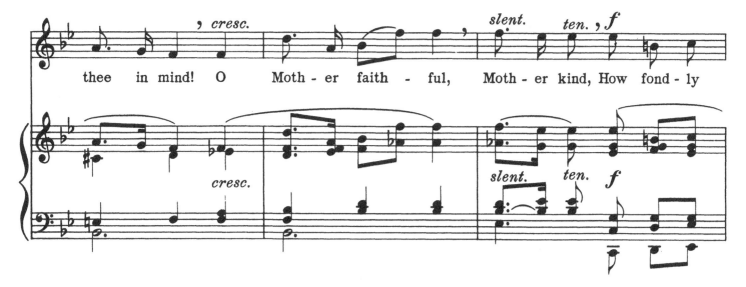

thee in mind! O Moth - er faith - ful, Moth - er kind, How fond - ly

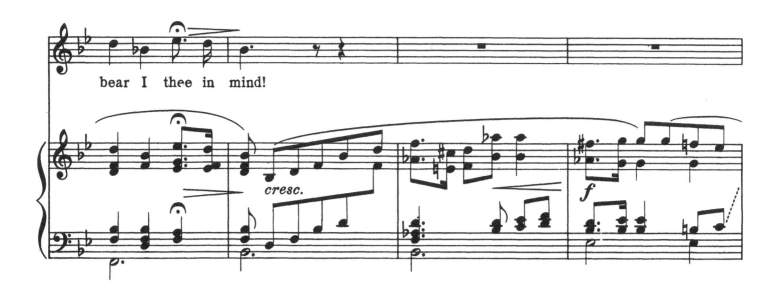

bear I thee in mind!

The in-fant soul thy love has guid-ed To vir-tue,

right and faith-ful-ness; All sin and shame my heart a-void-ed— Thou gav-est

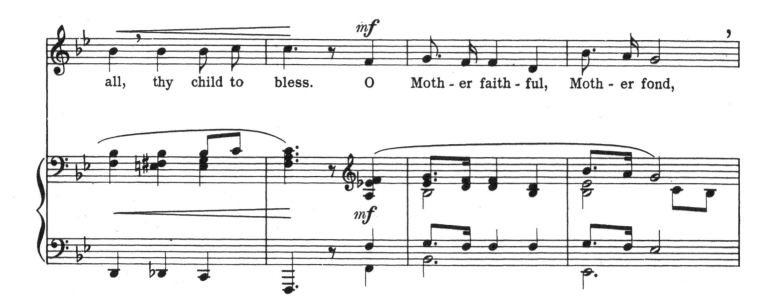

all, thy child to bless. O Moth-er faith-ful, Moth-er fond,

No joy I knew, thy love be-yond! O Moth - er faith - ful,

Moth - er fond, No joy I knew, thy love be - yond!

O may thy

bless - ing fail me nev - er, While yet a time I la - bor

here, And when all strife and toil are o - ver, May thy dear face my vi-sion

Man.                                                                          Ped.

cheer: Still shine up-on me, from a-bove, Thy ten-der gaze of

moth - er-love! Still shine up-on___ me, from a-bove, Thy ten - der

rit. molto        p lento

gaze of moth - er - love!

cresc.        dim.        mf        dim.        rall.

# My heart at thy sweet voice

## Mon cœur s'ouvre à ta voix

### from the opera "Samson et Dalila"

Camille Saint-Saëns

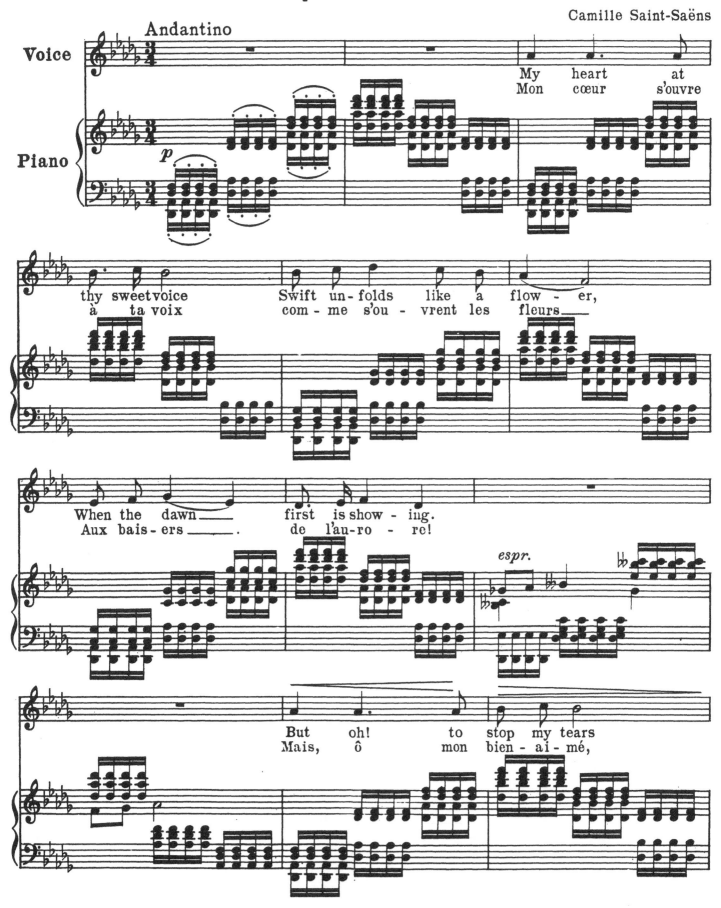

Printed in the U.S.A. by G. Schirmer, Inc.

woo - ing, Lis-ten\_\_\_ un-to my woo - ing. Ah \_\_\_\_ 'tis with
dres - se, Ré - ponds\_\_\_ à ma ten-dres - se! Ah! \_\_\_\_ ver-se-

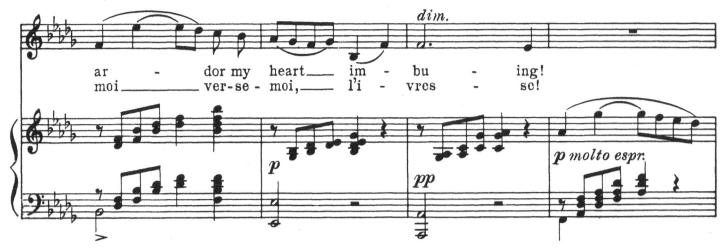

ar - dor my heart\_\_\_ im - bu - ing!
moi \_\_\_\_ ver-se - moi, l'i - vres - se!

As when a
Ain - si qu'on

And thus while love 'tis show - ing,
prêt à se con - so - ler,

To the voice 'tis tri - bute pay - ing.
A ta voix qui m'est che - re!

*rinf. poco animato*

An ar - row is less
La flè - che est moins ra-

*sf*

fleet That brings death in its
pide à por - ter le tré -

# „Mein gläubiges Herze, frohlocke."

"My heart ever faithful, sing praises."

JOHANN SEBASTIAN BACH.

lo-cke,　　sing',　　scherze, froh-lo - - - cke,sing',scher -
praises,　　be　　joy-ful, sing prais - - es, be joy- -

- - ze, mein gläu-bi-ges Her-ze,froh-lo - cke,sing',scher-ze, froh-
- ful, My heart_ev-er faith-ful,Sing prais - es, be joy-ful, sing

lo - cke,sing',scher - ze, dein Je - sus ist da!
prais - es, be joy - ful, Thy Je - sus is here!

# "My mother bids me bind my hair."

### (Bind' auf dein Haar.)

## Canzonet.

JOSEPH HAYDN.

moth-er— bids me bind—my hair With bands— of— ros- y hue, Tie
auf Dein Haar, die Mut-ter spricht, und Bän - der win - de drein; mit

up___ my sleeves with rib - ands rare, And lace my bod - ice blue,
ro - sen-ro - then Schleifen licht, so schmück'Dein Mie - der fein,

*fz*

Tie up___ my sleeves with rib - ands rare, And lace,___ and
mit ro - sen-ro - then Schlei-fen licht, so schmück', so

*fz*    *fz*

lace my_bod - ice blue.
schmück' Dein Mie-der_ fein.

For
Willst

why, she cries, sit still and weep, While oth - ers dance and
trau - ern Du, mein' Kind, al - lein, weil Al - les tanzt so

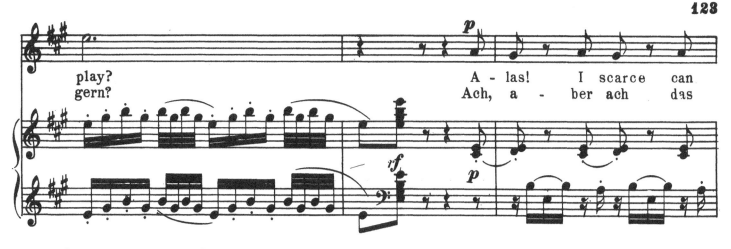

play?
gern?

A - las!    I scarce can
Ach,  a - ber ach   das

go    or creep,   While Lu - bin   is   a - way.                    A -
Her - ze mein    seufzt: weh!   mein Lieb' ist fern!                Ach,

las!   I scarce  can  go    or creep, while Lu - bin is   a - way,         while
a - ber ach,   das Her - ze mein seufzt: weh!   mein Lieb' ist fern!       mein

Lu - bin is a - way,    is    a - way,    is    a - way.
Lieb', mein Lieb' ist fern!   Ist   so fern!   Ist   so fern!

'Tis sad— to think the days are gone, When those— we love are near! I
O schö-ne Zeit, da Er—mir nah', den ein-zig ich— ge-liebt, ich

sit— up-on this mos-sy stone, And sigh when none can hear,
si-tze auf dem Stei-ne da und seuf-ze schwer be-trübt.

I sit— up-on this mos-sy stone, and sigh,— And sigh when none can
Ich si-tze auf dem Stei-ne da und seuf-ze, seuf—ze schwer be-

hear.
trübt.
And while I spin my
Ich spin—ne, doch ich

# My Old Kentucky Home, Good-Night

Words and Music by
Stephen C. Foster

1. The sun shines bright in the old Ken-tuck-y home, 'Tis
2. They hunt no more for the 'pos-sum and the 'coon On the
3. The head must bow and the back will have to bend, Wher-

sum-mer, the dark-ies are gay; The corn-top's ripe and the
mead-ow, the hill, and the shore; They sing no more by the
ev-er the dark-y may go; A few more days and the

mead-ow's in the bloom, While the birds make mu-sic all the day; The
glim-mer of the moon, On the bench by the old cab-in door: The
troub-le all will end, In the fields where the su-gar-canes grow; A

young folks roll on the lit-tle cab-in floor, All mer-ry, all hap-py, and bright, By'n'-
day goes by like a shadow o'er the heart, With sor-row where all was de-light, The
few more days for to tote the wea-ry load, No mat-ter, 'twill nev-er be light, A

by hard times comes a-knocking at the door, Then, my old Kentucky home, good-night!
time has come when the dark-ies have to part, Then, my old Kentucky home, good-night!
few more days till we tot-ter on the road, Then, my old Kentucky home, good-night!

**Chorus**

Soprano / Alto / Tenor / Bass:

Weep no more, my la-dy, Oh! weep no more to-day! We will sing one song for the old Kentucky home, For the old Kentucky home far a-way.

*D. S.*

# One Sweetly Solemn Thought

## Sacred Song

*Mezzo-Soprano or Baritone*

PHOEBE CARY

R. S. Ambrose

I am near - er home to-day Than I've ev - er____ been be -

fore. Near - er my Fa - ther's house, Where the

man - y man - sions be; Near - er the great white

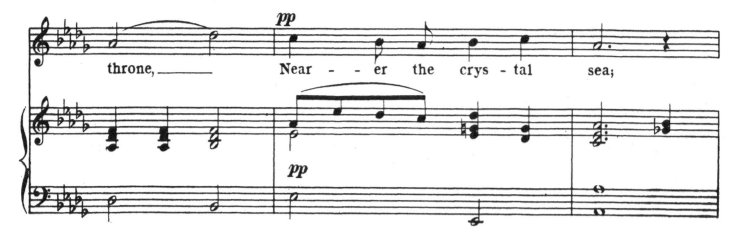

throne,____ Near - - er the crys - tal sea;

Near - er the bounds of life, Where we lay our bur - dens down; Near - er leav - ing the cross,_____ Near - er_____ gain - ing the crown. But ly - ing dark - ly be - tween,_____ Wind - ing a - down thro' the night,_____

Is the si - lent, un - known stream That leads_ at last to the

light. Fa - ther, be near when my feet Are

slip - ping o'er the brink, For it may be I am

near - er home, Near - er now than I think.

# „Nur, wer die Sehnsucht kennt"

## "One who has yearn'd, alone"

P. Tschaikowsky

Poem by Goethe
English version by
Dr. Th. Baker

Op. 6, No 6.
Original key.

Nur, wer die Sehn - sucht kennt, weiss, was ich lei - de!

One who has yearn'd, a - lone Can know my an - guish!

Al - lein und ab - ge - trennt von al - ler Freu - de,

Where ev - 'ry joy is flown For - lorn I lan - guish!

Seh' ich an's
'Tis on - ly

*un poco marcato*

Fir - ma - ment nach je - ner Sei - te. Ach! der mich
yon I see The skies a - bove___ me; Ah! far a-

liebt und kennt, ist in der Wei - te. Nur, wer die
way is he Who knows and loves me! One who has

Sehn - sucht kennt, weiss, was ich lei - de! Al - lein und
yearn'd, a - lone Can know my an - guish! Where ev - 'ry

ab - ge - trennt von al - - ler Freu - de, al - lein____ und ab - ge -
joy is flown For - lorn I lan - guish, Where ev - - 'ry joy is

trennt____ von al - ler Freu - de! Es schwindelt
flown____ For - lorn I lan - guish! With heart on

mir,____ es brennt mein Ein - - ge - wei - de, nur, wer die
fire____ I swoon In end - - less an - guish! One who has

Sehn - sucht kennt, weiss, was ich lei - de!
yearn'd, a - lone Knows how I lan - guish!

# O rest in the Lord

## Aria from the oratorio "Elijah"

Psalm XXXVII

Felix Mendelssohn
Edited by Carl Deis

87700

sires, \_\_\_ and He shall give thee thy heart's de - sires. Com-mit thy way un-

to Him, \_\_\_ and trust in Him; com-mit thy way un - to Him, \_\_\_ and trust in

Him, and fret\_ not thy - self \_\_\_ be-cause of e - vil do - ers. O rest in the

Lord, wait pa-tient-ly for Him, wait pa-tient-ly for Him; O rest in the

Lord wait pa-tient-ly for Him, and He shall give thee thy heart's de-

*cresc.*

sires,___ and He shall give___ thee thy heart's de - sires, and He shall

*sf*   *p*   *cresc.*   *sf*

give thee thy heart's de - sires. O rest in the Lord, O rest in the

*p*

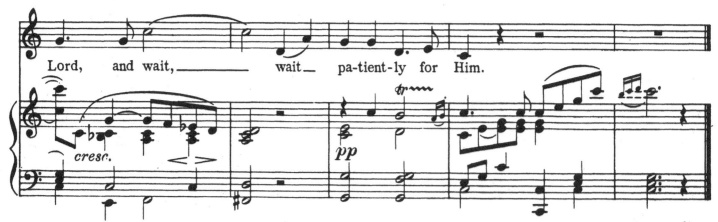

Lord, and wait,_____ wait__ pa-tient-ly for Him.

*cresc.*   *pp*

# 'O sole mio!

## My Sunshine

Poem by G. Capurro
English version by
Henry G. Chapman

E. di Capua

Che bel - la co - sa 'na iur - na - ta'e so - le._____ Ma n'a-tu
Oh! what's so fine, dear, As a day of sun - shine?_____ An-oth-er

so - le_____ cchiù bel-lo, ohi - nè,_____ 'o so - le mi - o_____ sta 'nfron-te a
sun - light_____ Far love-lier lies,_____ Oh my own sun - shine!_ In your dear

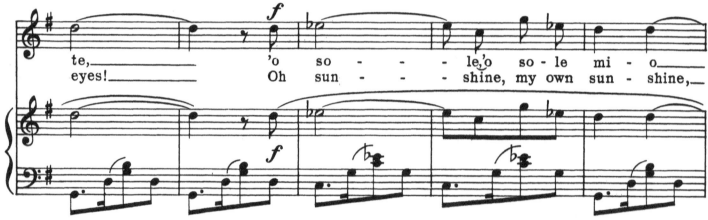

te,_____ 'o so - - - le, 'o so - le mi - o_____
eyes!_____ Oh sun - - - shine, my own sun - shine,

_ sta 'nfron-te a te,_____ sta 'nfron-te a te!_____
_ In your dear eyes,_____ in your dear eyes!_____

# La Paloma
## The Dove

**English version by**
**Henry G. Chapman**

S. Yradier

1. The day_____ that I left Ha - ba - na, (The Lord be praised!)
2. But now_____ we shall soon be mar - ried, (The Lord be praised!)

1. Cuan - do_____ sa - li de la Ha - ba - na, ¡Val - ga - me Dios!
2. El dia_____ que nos ca - se - mos, ¡Val - ga - me Dios!

Not one___ came to see me off,___ Ex-cept my-self,___
One week___ it will soon be gone, I laugh for joy.___

Na - die___ me ha vis-to sa - lir,___ Si - no fui yo,___
En la___ se - ma - na que hay ir___ me ha ce re - ir.___

And one___ pret-ty Mex - i - ca - na: But what cared we?___
And when___ at the church we've tar-ried, The knot to tie,___

Yu - na___ lin - da Gau-chi-nan-ga A - llà voy yo,___
Des - de___ lay-gle-sia jun - ti-tos, Que si se - ñor,___

Who came,___ well in fact just came_ A - long with me.
We'll look___ for a place to sleep_(And what care I!)

Que se___ vi - no tras de mi,___ Que si se - ñor.
Nos i -___ re-mos a dor-mir,___ A - llá voy yo.

1-2. If to thy win-dow ev-er shall come a wee dove,_____
1-2. Si á tu ven-ta-na lle-ga u-na Pa-lo-ma,_____

Treat it with kind-ness, for thou wilt find 'tis me, love,_____
Tra-ta-la con ca-ri-ño, que es mi per-so-na,_____

Tell it thy love, ah! tell it thy love for me, dear!_____
Cuen-ta-la tus a-mo-res, bien de mi vi-da,_____

Crown it with flow'rs, be-cause it has come to thee, dear._____ Do, my dar-ling, I pray!
Co-ro-na-la de flo-res, que es co-sa mi-a._____ ¡Ay! chi-ni-ta que si,

Thou must give me thy love, ah!_____ So come with me, come with me, dar-ling,
¡ay! que da-me tu a-mor, ¡ay!_____ Que ven - te con - mi - go chi - ni - ta

come with me where I dwell! Do, my dar-ling, I pray! Thou must give me thy
a - dón - de vi - vo yo. ¡Ay! chi - ni - ta que si, ¡ay! que da-me tu a-

love, ah!_____ So come with me, come with me, dar - ling, come with me where I
mor, ¡ay!_____ Que ven - te con - mi - go chi - ni - ta a - dón - de vi - vo

**1.** dwell! **2.** dwell!
yo. yo.

# Passing By

Anonymous poem from
Thomas Ford's
*Musicke of Sundrie Kinds* (1607)

Edward Purcell
Piano accompaniment by Carl Deis

37700

**Poco più di movimento** ♩ circa 84

Her ges-ture, mo - tion and her smiles, Her wit, her voice my

heart___ be-guiles, Be-guiles my heart, I know not why, And

yet I love her till I die.

Come prima

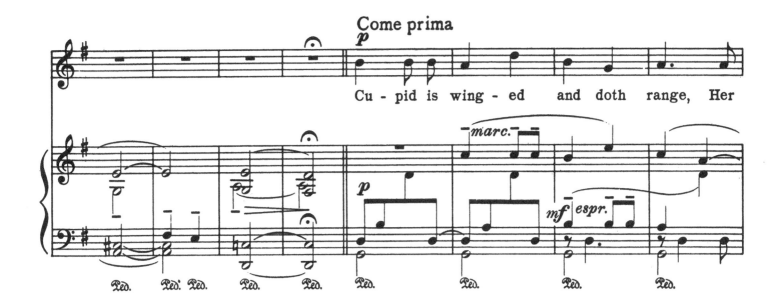

Cu - pid is wing - ed and doth range, Her

coun - try so my love___ doth change, But change she earth or

change she sky, Yet will I love her till I die.

# Obstination

(François Coppée)

## A Resolve

H. de FONTENAILLES

Andantino. (♩ = 72)

Voice

Vous aurez beau faire et beau
It is all in vain to im-

Piano

di — re!
plore me

L'ou-bli me se-rait o - di - eux,
Not to let her im - age be - guile,

Et je vois toujours son sou - ri - re Des a - dieux,
For her face is ev - er be - fore me, And her smile,

des a -
and her

87700

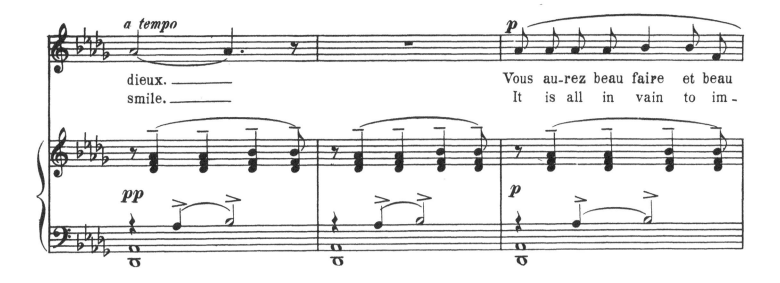

a tempo

dieux. _____
smile. _____

*p*

Vous au-rez beau faire et beau
It is all in vain to im-

*pp*
*p*

di _ re,
plore me

Dût el _ le-mê-me l'i-gno-rer:
All thoughts of her a-way to keep,

*f*                                        *rit.*                                      *pp*

Je veux, fi-dèle à mon mar-ty _ _ re, La pleu-rer, _____ la pleu-
For still, although she may ig-nore        me, I can weep, _____ I can

*colla parte*        *ten.*   *colla parte*

*f*

Vous au-rez beau dire et beau fai - re,
It is all in vain to en - treat me

Seule, el - le peut mon mal gué - rir,
Mem - o - ry's pow - er to de - fy,

Et j'ai - me mieux, s'il per - sé -
For if she will - eth to de -

vè - re, En mou - rir, _____ en mou - rir.
feat me, I can die, _____ I can die. (Constance Bache.)

# Sapphische Ode

(Hans Schmidt)

## Sapphic Ode

Edited by Max Spicker
English version by
Henry G. Chapman

Johannes Brahms
Op. 94, No 4

**Ziemlich langsam**
*Poco lento*

Ro - sen brach ich nachts mir am dunk - len Ha - ge;
Ros - es I at night from the hedge did sev - er,

sü - sser hauch - ten Duft sie, als je ___ am Ta - ge,
Sweet - er scent they breathed than in day - time ev - er;

doch ver
Yet the

streu - ten reich die be - weg - ten Ae - ste
branch - es when I dis - turbed them threw me

Thau, ___ der mich
Drops ___ to be -

näss - ___ - te.
dew ___ me.

37700

Auch der Küs - se Duft mich wie nie be - rück - te,
Ne'er have scent - ed kiss - es my heart so shak - en,

die ich nachts vom Strauch dei-ner Lip - pen pflück - te: doch auch
As have those by night from thy lips__ I've tak - en. Yet thou

dir, be-wegt im Ge - müth__gleich je - nen, thau - - - ten die
too wert moved when my kiss - es wooed thee, Tear - - drops be -

Thrä - - - nen.
dew'd_____ thee.

# Ständchen

(Rellstab)

## Serenade

English version by
Henry G. Chapman

Franz Schubert

Lei - se fle - hen mei - ne Lie - der durch die Nacht zu dir,
Soft - ly goes my song's en-trea - ty Thro' the night to thee,

in — den stil - len Hain her-nie - der,
In — the si - lent woods I wait thee,

Lieb - chen, komm zu mir.
Come, my love,— to me.

Flü-sternd schlan - ke Wip-fel rau - schen in — des Mon - des Licht,
Tree-tops slen - der sough and whis - per In — the moon - light here,

in — des Mon - des Licht, des Ver - rä - thers feind-lich Lau - schen
in — the moon - light here, No un-friend - ly ear shall lis - ten,

fürch - te, Hol - de, nicht, fürch - te, Hol - de, nicht.
Dar - ling, have no fear, dar - ling, have no fear.

Hörst die Nach - ti - gal - len schla-gen? Ach! sie fle - hen dich,
Hark! the night - in - gales are sing - ing, Ah, they plead with thee!

mit der Tö - ne sü - ssen Kla - gen
With their notes so sweet, so ring - ing,

fle - hen sie für mich.
They would plead for me.

Sie ver-steh'n des Bu-sens Seh - nen, ken-nen Lie - bes-schmerz,
Well they know a lov-er's long - ing, Know the pain of love,

*pp*

ken - nen Lie - bes-schmerz, rüh-ren mit den Sil-ber-tö - nen
know the pain of love, With their sil - ver-ton-ed voic - es

je - des wei - che Herz, je - des wei - che Herz.
Ten - der hearts they move, ten - der hearts they move.

Lass auch dir die Brust be-we - gen, Lieb - chen, hö - re mich!
Ah, let thine, as well, grow ten - der, Sweet - heart, why so coy?

*cresc.*

be - bend harr' ich dir ent-ge - gen,
An - xious, fe - ver'd, I a-wait thee,

komm, be - glü - cke mich! komm, be - glü - cke mich,____
Come and bring me joy, come and bring me joy,____

be - glü - cke mich!
and bring me joy!

Poem by W. Henzen,
after the Norwegian of H. Ibsen.
English version by Dr. Th. Baker.

# Solvejg's Lied.

## Solvejg's Song.

Edvard Grieg

Un poco andante.

har - re treu-lich dein, ich har - re treu-lich dein. (vor sich hin summend.) Ah!
wait-ing, ev - er thine, I'm wait-ing, ev - er thine! (humming to herself.) Ah!

hel - fe dir, wenn du die Son - ne noch siehst, die Son - ne noch siehst, Gott
help thee, whil - ev - er His sun thou dost feel, His sun thou dost feel, God

seg-ne dich, wenn du zu Fü - ssen ihm kniest, zu Fü - ssen ihm kniest.
bless thee, when-e'er at His feet thou dost kneel, at His feet thou dost kneel.

# Chanson indoue

## A Song of India

### FROM THE LEGEND "SADKO"

Transl. from the original Russian
by H. Cecil Cowdrey

N. Rimsky - Korsakow

Thy hid-den gems are rich be-yond all
*Les di - a - mants chez nous sont in - nom-*

mea - sure, Un - num-bered are the pearls thy wa - ters trea - sure, Oh won - drous
*bra - bles; Les per - les dans nos mers in - cal - cu - la - bles; C'est l'In - de,*

land! Oh land of In - dia!
*ter - re des mer - veil - les.*
Where_____ the
*Dans_____ un*

*pp sempre legato assai*

sea_____ en - clos - es
*de_____ nos si - - tes_____*
Cliffs_____ with ru - - bies
*Un_____ ru - bis_____ é -*

la - - den,_____
*mer - - - ge._____*
Phoe - - nix there_____ re - pos - - -
*Un_____ oi - seau_____ l'ha - bi - -*

es,_____
*te,_____*
Bird_____ with face_____ of maid - - - en._____
*Au_____ vi - sa - ge de vier - - - ge!_____*

Sweet___ the ca-dence fall - - ing,___
*Jour___ et nuit il chan - - - - te___*

Pa - ra - dise re - call - - - ing;___
*D'u - ne voix ra - vis - san - - - te;___*

Gold - - en plumes___ ad - vanc - - - ing___
*Son___ bril - lant___ plu - ma - - - ge___*

Hide___ the rip - - ples danc - - ing;___
*Cou - - vre tout___ le ri - va - - ge,___*

He_____ who hears_____ that sing - - er___ Shall_____ for -
Qui____ pour - rait_____ l'en - ten - - dre,____ Re - - naî -

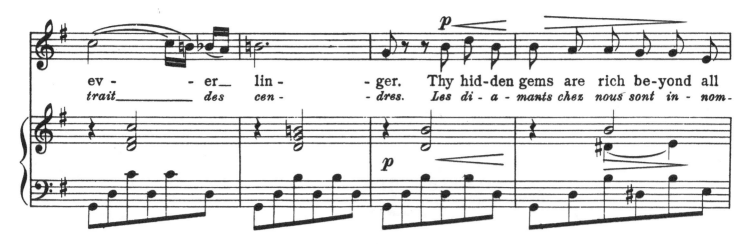

ev - - er lin - - ger. Thy hid-den gems are rich be-yond all
trait_____ des cen - - dres. Les di - a - mants chez nous sont in - nom -

dream - ing, Be-neath thy waves un - num-bered pearls lie gleam - ing, Oh won-drous
bra - bles, Les per - les dans nos mers in - cal - cu - la - bles; C'est l'In - de,

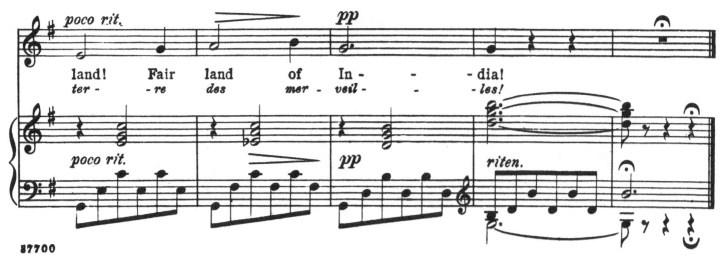

land! Fair land of In - - dia!
ter - - re des mer - veil - - - les!

poco rit.

pp

riten.

# Song of the Volga Boatmen

Russian words in
phonetic spelling

English version by
Sigmund Spaeth

Harmonized by
Carl Deis

# „Als die alte Mutter"
## "Songs my mother taught me"

English version by
NATALIE MACFARREN

Andante con moto

Anton Dvořák. Op. 55, № 4.

Als die _ al - te _ Mut - - ter
Songs my _ moth-er _ taught me

mich noch _ lehr - te _ sin - - gen,
in the _ days long _ van - - ish'd;

Thrä - nen in _ den _
Sel - dom from her _

Wim - - pern gar so oft ihr hin - - gen.
eye - - lids were the tear - drops ban - - ish'd.

87700

Jetzt, wo_ ich die_ Klei -
Now I_ teach my_ chil -

nen sel - ber_ üb' im_ San - - ge, rie - selt's
dren each me - lo - dious_ meas - - ure; Oft the

in den_ Bart_____ oft, rie - selt's oft_____ von der
(mir_ vom_ Au - - ge, rie - selts oft mir_ auf die
tears_ are_ flow - - ing, oft they flow_____ from my

brau - nen_ Wan - - ge.
brau - ne_ Wan - - ge.)
mem - ry's_ treas - ure.

# Sylvelin

English version by
F. H. Martens

Christian Sinding. Op.55, I

Syl-velin, God's own blessing be on you the whole day through!
Syl-velin, seg-ne Gott Dich auf Er-den zu je-der Stund'!

Blue eyes, and skin so white, and red the mouth of you.— As
Dein Aug' ist blau, Dein Ant-litz licht und roth Dein Mund. Wie

sun- -beams up- on the meadow, when morn drives the gloom of night,
Son- -nen-schein auf den Fel-dern, Des Mor-gens nach lan-ger Nacht

27700

You have brought cheer to my mind opprest, my sorrowful heart made light.
Hast Du er - hellt mir den dunklen Sinn, mich Trauri-gen froh ge-macht.

Syl - ve-lin, Syl-velin, in all my prayers at night I remember
Syl - ve-lin, Syl-velin! Allnächtlich schliess' ich in mein Ge-bet Dich

you;
ein.

God's blessing be on you ev - er, He
Gott seg-ne Dich al - le Ta - ge, er

knows your heart is true.
weiss: Dein Herz ist rein.

# Then you'll remember me

## from the opera "The Bohemian Girl"

Alfred Bunn

M. W. Balfe

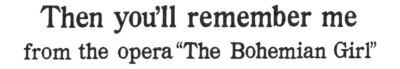

When oth - er lips and

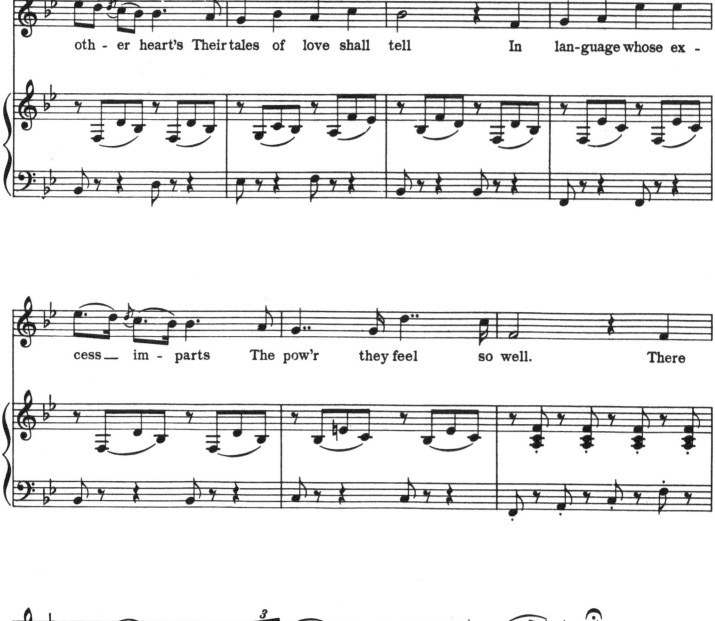

oth - er heart's Their tales of love shall tell In lan-guage whose ex -

cess__ im - parts The pow'r they feel so well. There

may per-haps in such__ a__ scene Some re - col - lec - tion be, Of

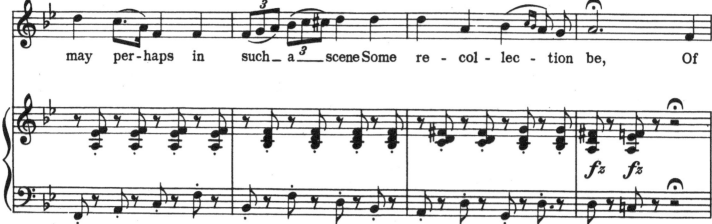

days that have as hap-py been, And you'll re - mem - ber me, _____ And you'll re -

mem-ber, you'll re-mem - ber me.

When cold-ness or de - ceit shall slight The

beau -ty now they prize, And deem it but a fa - ded light Which

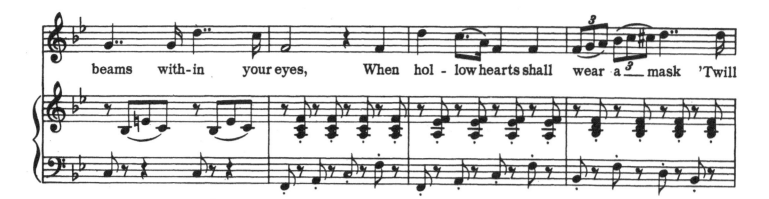

beams with-in your eyes, When hol - low hearts shall wear a mask 'Twill

break your own to see, In such a mo - ment I but ask That

you'll re - mem - ber me, That you'll re - mem - ber, you'll re - mem - ber me.

# Du bist wie eine Blume
## Thou art so like a flower

Heinrich Heine

Robert Schumann, Op. 25, No. 24
Composed 1840
Edited by Carl Deis

ist,_____ als ob ich die Hän - de — Auf's Haupt dir le - gen
fain_____ would lay,_ in bless-ing, — My hands up-on_____ thy

sollt', — Be-tend, dass Gott dich er-hal-te — So rein und schön und
brow, — Pray-ing that God may e'er keep thee — As pure and fair as

hold.
now.

# To You

## Zueignung

(Hermann v. Gilm)

**English version by
Dr. Th. Baker**

Richard Strauss. Op. 10, No. 1

Copyright, 1916, by G. Schirmer, Inc.
Copyright renewed, 1944, by G. Schirmer, Inc.

Till    your love          I knew,    my    own,
und     du  seg - - ne - test    den    Trank,

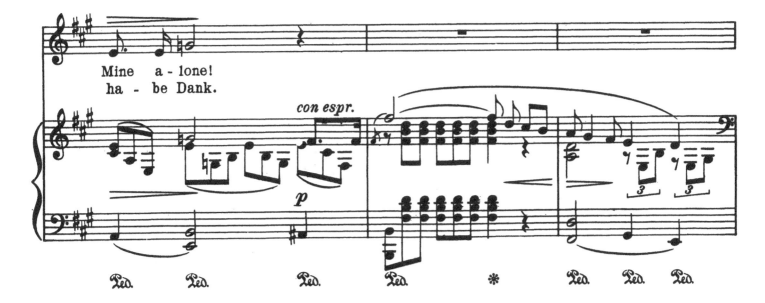

Mine  a - lone!
ha - be Dank.

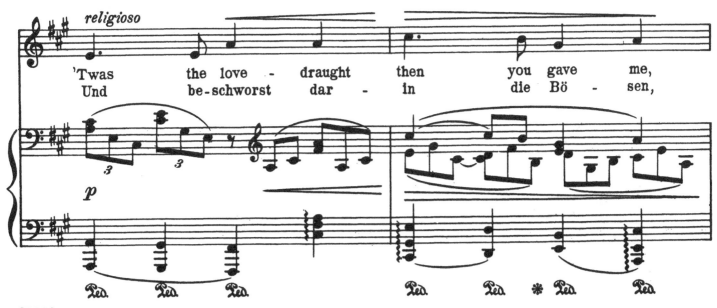

'Twas      the love   draught    then      you gave      me,
Und        be-schworst    dar - in      die Bö - sen,

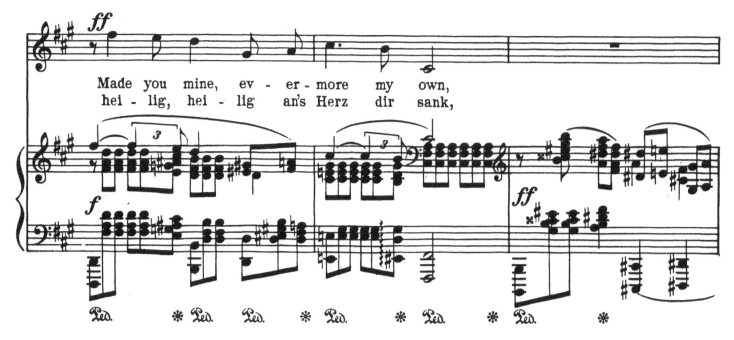

# Die beiden Grenadiere
## The Two Grenadiers

English version by
Henry G. Chapman

Robert Schumann

Nach Frank-reich zo-gen zwei Gre-na-
For France were making two gren-a-

dier', die wa-ren in Russ-land ge-fan-gen, und
diers, From pris-on in Rus-sia re-turn-ing, And

als sie ka-men in's deut-sche Quar-tier, sie lie-ssen die Kö-pfe
when to Ger-ma-ny's quar-ters they came, They hung their heads in

han-gen, da hör-ten sie bei-de die trau-ri-ge Mähr', dass
mourn-ing; 'Twas there that the sor-row-ful sto-ry they heard, How

Frank - reich ver - lo - ren ge - gan - gen, be - siegt und ge - schla - gen das
France had been crushed and for - sak - en, Her glo - ri - ous ar - mies de -

ta - pfe - re Heer und der Kai - ser, der Kai - ser ge - fan - gen!
feat - ed and slain, And the Em - p'ror, the Em - p'ror was tak - en!

Da wein - ten zu - sammen die Gre - na - dier,' wohl ob ___ der kläg - li - chen
Then wept they to - geth - er, those gren - a - diers, These dole - ful ti - dings at

Kun - de; der Ei - ne sprach: „Wie weh wird mir, wie brennt mei - ne al - - te
learn - ing; Then quoth the one: "My tears are hot, But hot - ter my old wound is

Wun-de!" Der And're sprach: „Das Lied ist aus, auch ich möcht' mit dir ster-ben, doch
burn-ing!" The oth-er said: "The end has come, My life I'd glad-ly of-fer, But

hab' ich Weib und Kind zu Haus, die oh - ne mich ver - der - ben." „Was schert mich
I've a wife and child at home, Who but for me would suf-fer." "Who cares for

Weib? was schert mich Kind? ich tra - ge weit bess'-res Ver-
wife? who cares for child? My pit - y they do not

lan - gen, lass sie bet-teln geh'n, wenn sie hung-rig sind, mein
wak - en, Let them go and beg, if they're hun-gry, man! My

Kai - ser, mein Kai - ser ge - fan - gen! Ge - währ' mir, Bru - der, ei - ne
Em - p'ror, my Em - p'ror is tak - en! One prom - ise, com-rade, you must

Bitt', wenn ich jetzt ster - ben wer - de, so
make, If this hard blow should slay me, To

nimm mei - ne Lei - che nach Frank-reich mit, be - grab' mich in Frank - reichs
car - ry my bod - y back to France, And un - der her soil to

Er - de, das Eh - ren-kreuz am ro - then Band
lay me; And when my cross on its scar-let band

sollst du auf's Herz mir    le - gen,        die Flin - te gieb mir in die
O - ver my heart you've    bound me,        Then put    my mus-ket in my

Hand,            und gürt' mir um    den De - gen.    So
hand            And belt    my sword    a - round me.    So

will    ich lie - gen und    hor - chen still, wie    ei -    ne Schild - wach' im
shall    I    lie there and    lis - ten aye, A    sen - ti - nel 'midst the

Gra - be,            bis    einst ich hö - re Ka - no - nen-ge - brüll    und
cors - es,            Un - til the rum - ble of    can - non I hear,    The

wie - hern-der Ros - se Ge - tra - be;     dann    rei - tet mein Kai - ser wohl
neigh of the tramp-ling hors - es!     'Twill    mean that the Em - p'ror rides

ü - ber mein Grab, viel Schwer - ter klir - ren und bli - tzen, viel Schwer-ter klir - ren und
o - ver my grave, With sa - bres flash-ing in splendor, with sa - bres flash-ing in

bli - tzen;     dann    steig' ich ge - waff - net her - vor aus dem Grab, den
splen-dor,     Then    armed for the fray from my grave will I spring, And

Kai - ser, den Kai - ser zu schü - tzen!"       Adagio
rise as my Em-p'ror's de - fend - er!"

# Das Veilchen.

(Goethe.)

## The Violet.

English version by
Dr. Th. Baker.

W. A. MOZART.

Allegretto.

Ein Veil-chen auf der Wie-se stand, in sich ge-bückt und

A vio-let on the mead-ow grew, So all a-lone, and

un-be-kannt; es war ein her-zig's Veil-chen! Da kam ein' jun-ge

low-ly too, It was a dar-ling vi-o-let! There came a youth-ful

Schä-fe-rin mit leich-tem Schritt und mun-ter'm Sinn da-her! da

shep-herd-ess, With step so light, and heart no less, And sang, and

her! die Wie-se_ her, und_ sang.
sang while o'er the_ mead she_ pass'd.

*dolce*

Ach, denkt das Veil-chen,_ wär' ich
Ah! thought the vi-o-let,_ might I_

nur die schön-ste Blu-me der Na-tur, ach! nur_____ ein klei-nes
be The fair-est blos-som on the lea, If on--ly_ for a

*fp*

Weil-chen! Bis mich das Lieb-chen ab-ge-pflückt, und an dem Bu-sen
while yet! Till found by her I love, and press'd All faint-ing on her

Till mich das Lieb-chen

matt ge-drückt, ach nur! ach nur ein Vier-tel-stünd-chen lang!
ten-der breast, Tho' e'en, tho' e'en that mo-ment were my last!

*ff*

# Were my song with wings provided

## Si mes vers avaient des ailes

Victor Hugo
English version by
Dr. Th. Baker

Reynaldo Hahn

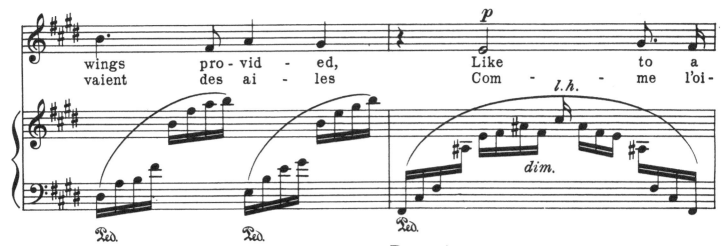

wings pro - vid - ed, Like to a
vaient des ai - les Com - me l'oi-

Poco più mosso

bird! Un-to the air so con-
seau! Ils vo-le-raient, é - tin-

fid - - ed, Would thy cham-ber be its
cel - - les, Vers vo-tre foy-er qui

goal,_____ Were my song with wings pro - vid - ed,
rit,_____ Si mes vers a - vaient des ai - les

# Hoffnung.

### "When the roses bloom."

Louise Reichardt.
(1778–1825.)

Einfach und innig, die 2te Strophe mit dem Ausdruck der Verklärung.
*Semplice con affetto, la 2da strofa con espress. beatificata.*

Wenn die Ro - sen blü - hen, hof - fe, lie - bes Herz,
In the time of ros - es, Hope, thou wear - y heart!

still und kühl ver - glü - hen wird der hei - sse Schmerz.
Spring a balm dis - clos - es For the keen - est smart.

Was den Win - ter ü - ber oft _____ un-heil - bar schien,
Tho' thy grief _____ o'er - come thee Thro' _____ the win - ter's gloom,

es ent-weicht das Fie - ber, wenn die Ro - sen blüh'n.
Thou shalt thrust it from thee, When the ros - es bloom.

Wenn die Ro - sen blü - hen, matt ge - quäl - tes Herz,
In the time of ros - es, Wear - y heart, re - joice!

*pp*

freu - e dich! wir zie - hen dann wohl him - mel - wärts.
Ere the sum - mer clos - es Comes the longed-for Voice.

E - wig dann _____ ge - ne - sen, wirst _____ du neu er - glüh'n,
Let not death _____ ap - pal thee, For, _____ be-yond the tomb,

*espress.*     *poco sostenuto*

wirst ein himm - lisch We - sen, wenn die Ro - - sen blüh'n.
God Him - self shall call thee, When the ros - - es bloom.

*fz*

# Where'er you walk

## Aria from "Semele"

Edited by H. Heale

G. F. Händel

# Whispering Hope

Alice Hawthorne

Whis - per-ing, whis-per - ing Hope,____ oh, how wel - come thy

voice, how wel - - come, Mak - ing my heart in its

sor - - row re - joice,____ re - joice.____

D.C.

Voice

Piano

Moderato

*p*

*p dolce*

1. Soft as the voice of an an - gel, Breath-ing a les - son un -
2. If, in the dusk of the twi - light, Dim be the re - gion a -

*p*

heard,____ Hope, with a gen - tle per - sua - sion,
far,____ Will not the deep - en - ing dark - ness

87700

87700

Whis - pers her com-fort-ing word.＿ Wait, till the dark-ness is o - ni-
Bright - en the glim-mer-ing star?＿ Then when the night is up - on

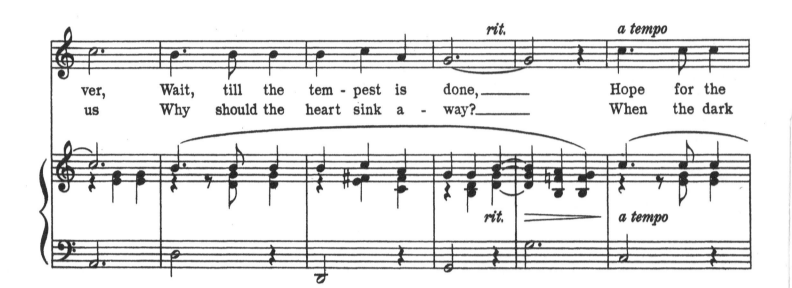

*rit.*      *a tempo*

ver, Wait, till the tem - pest is done,＿ Hope for the
us Why should the heart sink a - way?＿ When the dark

*rit.*     *a tempo*

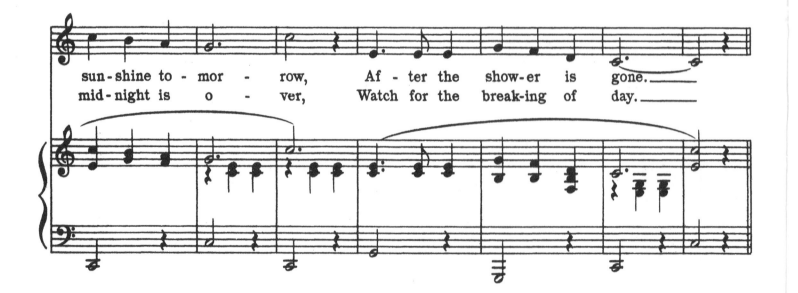

sun-shine to - mor - row, Af - ter the show-er is gone.＿
mid-night is o - ver, Watch for the break-ing of day.＿

**Refrain**

1-2.Whis - per - ing, whis-per - ing Hope,＿ oh, how wel - come thy

voice, how wel - come, Mak - ing my heart in its

sor - row re - joice,＿ re - joice.＿

*Ped.*

# Whispering Hope

Alice Hawthorne

1.Soft as the voice of an an - gel, Breath-ing a les - son un -
2. If, in the dusk of the twi - light, Dim be the re - gion a -

heard, _____ Hope, with a gen - tle per - sua - sion,
far, _____ Will not the deep - en - ing dark - ness

**Refrain**

1-2. Whis-per-ing, whis-per-ing Hope, _____ oh, how wel-come thy

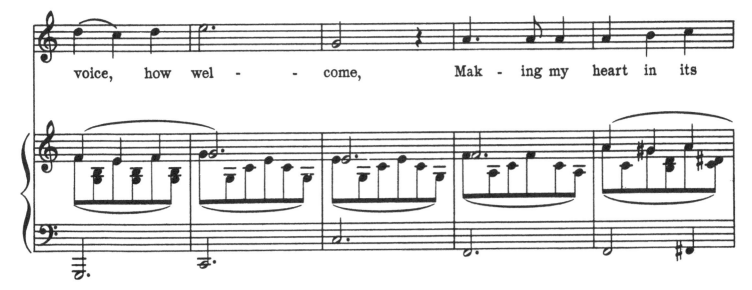

voice, how wel - - come, Mak - ing my heart in its

sor - - row re - joice, _____ re - joice. _____